*In celebration of my long dead father
and the conversations we might have had.*

The Muted Blade

Jean Andrews

Published 2017 by arima publishing

www.arimapublishing.com

ISBN 978 1 84549 *** *

© Jean Andrews 2017

All rights reserved

This book is copyright. Subject to statutory exception and to provisions of relevant collective licensing agreements, no part of this publication may be reproduced, stored in a retrieval system, or transmitted in any form or by any means, without the prior written permission of the author.

Printed and bound in the United Kingdom

This book is sold subject to the conditions that it shall not, by way of trade or otherwise, be lent, re-sold, hired out, or otherwise circulated without the publisher's prior consent in any form of binding or cover other than that which it is published and without a similar condition including this condition being imposed on the subsequent purchaser.

arima publishing
ASK House, Northgate Avenue
Bury St Edmunds, Suffolk IP32 6BB
t: (+44) 01284 700321

www.arimapublishing.com

Acknowledgements

'Planes' appeared in a slightly different form in Poetry Monthly in 2003.

Contents

Heritage — 13

I

Planes — 17
Thetford — 18
The March — 19
Another Day — 21
Never Forget — 22
Three Graces — 24
The One from Tikrit — 26
Plaza Mayor, Madrid — 27
Attack — 29
Paddy's Day — 30
Their Day — 32
Lest We Forget... — 33
Children's Homes — 34
The Gables — 35
D-Day, 60 Years On — 36
The Gipper — 37
Nancy — 38
Innisfree — 39
St Stephen's Day Tsunami — 41
Car Nicobar — 42
Promenade des Anglais — 43

Laois	44
Auschwitz	45
Tracheotomy	46
April Fools' Day, Valencia	47
Benedict XVI	48
Emeritus	49
Bologna	50
Woburn Place	51
7/7	52
The News	53
Georgie	54
This Year's Tree	55
Ceaucescu	56
Authority	57
South Beirut	58
Mao's Long March	59
John Lennon	60
The Fall	61
Assassination	62
Hafner's Paradise	63
A Guest of the Bishops	64
Intervention	66
Harry Patch	67
Stevo	68
Another Thirty-Three	69
Traitor in Gaza	70
The Children of Gaza	71
Plenipotentiary	73

II

Words and Music	77
Newstead Abbey	79
Acre	81
Clonmacnoise	82
Seán Buí	83
Little Things	84
A Beach in Fife	86
Bonnington	87
The Venice of Savoy	88
Spire	90
Pilgrimage	91
Portico	92
Veneziana	93
Turner in Venice	94
Stratford	95
A Room in the Prado, Now Dispersed	96
Dublin Grey	97
Rupprecht and Fergal	98
Rock of Ages	100
Gabriel	101
Church Militant	102
Destiny	104
Discovery	106
The Stars Look Down	108
The Gellért	110
Sentries	112

III

Sunflowers	117
Actor	118
The Higher Forms	119
Waltz	120
Releasing	121
Lost at Sea	122
The Bosphorus	123
Love	124
Generations	125
Remnants	126
Sevvy	127
Rugby For Your Country	129
Catnap	130
Monsters	131
16.06.2012	132
Quill	133
Edna O'Brien	134
Imbolc	135

Heritage

23rd March 2008, Easter Sunday

My father and I
had girded on our axes
to protect the dying
and the weak.

Then I heard the muted blade
of the alarm clock click,
destroying sleep.

I

'If we say that we have no sin, we deceive ourselves,
and the truth is not in us.'

Penitential Service for the first day of Lent,
Common Prayer.

Planes

4th August 2002
i.m. Eileen Barker

Every time
I hear an engine in the sky,
I remember what happened
when they said we lost our innocence.

We had it in full technicolour sound,
we knew the act of calculated malice
for what it was:
blood on blood,
the lives of those in the planes,
the lives of those on the ground.

It shocked us to our marrow,
as it was meant to.

But recently, I met a long-lost cousin
who had lived through London in the Blitz;
I saw, on her soft-skinned, unlined face
the ghost of what had been necessary for survival
and the lives of children.

In view of all of this,
I could only genuflect
and keep a dumbstruck peace.

Thetford

> i.m. Holly Wells and Jessica Chapman,
> d. 4th August 2002

Curious that I,
in this year of loss,
should be one of the many oblivious
on a leafy, sunny day,
to drive across that park.

Strange that a gamekeeper,
one controlling vermin,
inured to carrion carcasses of his own making,
protector of the vulnerable prey,
should find them.

Hard to take,
imperious nonetheless,
the random strike of a hidden claw,
the atavism of homicide
on the young.

The March

24th February 2003

The day we first talked politics
was the day of the march
against war on Iraq.
We should have gone,
but I had a briefcase
and you had things to do,
so we crossed it
on Tottenham Court Road,
like a pair of tourists,
macheteless in a jungle of eyes,
mottoes, klaxons and ears,
on police advice, solicited
courteously by you.

She addressed you as 'sir'
though you might have been coshed
in earlier, less tolerant times
— but not by a woman constable, mind —
and I held my tongue.
For my accent might have betrayed
even her, if no longer me,
as I have been mocked before now, repeatedly,
by those who think
they are observing a simple truth
— the norm of my nation's idiocy;
and you would have been taken in,
roughed up, then dumped in the gutter,
that place your Wildean ilk crawled out of
to stain their wholesome soil.

Even now, a decade and more further on,
such scenarios are not so far off the boil
that we can take their obsolescence for granted;
much as we would wish for them to constitute
no more than risible, unwonted calumny.

Another Day

20th May 2003

Twenty months after
the eleventh of September,
I had another day,
not of towers collapsing
in clouds of soot and ash,
more like being sucked back down
to my own feet of clay.

A past of grey, drenched
pebbledash walls
— these were the only walls;
sodden duffle coats piled high
in the corner of a lecture-room,
steam rising off them with a stench
of wet, yard-dwelling dogs
— these were the only coats;
male perspiration, synthetic-shod feet,
stale cigarette smoke, rancid beer
and dutiful, convent-school girls
— these were our only peers.

I never thought
that liberation from these norms
would collect its toll one day
in plaguing of the heart uncharted
in dry stone walls
and bogs of yellow gorse.

Never Forget

5th June 2003

Coventry Cathedral
with its *Father Forgive Them*,
the cross of burnt embers,
once proud rafters
ephemeral and blent with the sky,
the broad arch of the windows,
open reach to the heavens,
rent by air-mines
from across the North Sea
on a clear November night
in nineteen forty;
there were almost five hundred,
each one a casualty.

The Twin Towers:
nothing but mesh remained,
a crater called Ground Zero
and nearly three thousand
untimely in their graves.

Dresden, stone by numbered stone
— once only the Frauenkirche left,
with Luther on a plinth outside
in supplication,
abstracted, still a sentinel —
now finally given its redress;
those monumental Teuton warriors,
gnarled as the trunks of trees
and hewn from the same rock
that turned black and melted

into shapelessness
in the blast inferno
that night in February
nineteen forty-five,
when the firestorm was so severe
the inscription in the graveyard
could only state: 'how many dead?'

These are merely three
of thousands without number.
They are in our memory, there was flesh
on their scarified, sacrificed bones
though this will not persuade us to be better
or hesitate before we move again,
like lightening,
to unsheathe the claymore sword.

Three Graces

> 16th October 2003
> '...and the stars resound'.
> (Vicente Aleixandre, *To Fray Luis de León*)

These I have seen
in the past, short while:
each of them blond,
each of them sinuous,
each of them with a secret smile.

One I found at a meeting,
one in the jamb of a door,
one as he doused himself in a cult aroma
amid the perfume shelves
on the Duty Free floor.

The scent of Hugo Boss,
a seraph and his few surreptitious puffs
on the quarter-century anniversary
of a dying, embattled gatekeeper,
habemus papam, the skiing Pope.
An old man enduring arthritis, Parkinson's,
the encroachments of age,
salted away in Rome,
a poet, a mystic, a generous soul,
who in his day job
would not admit such angels
to their patrimony once more.

He has since been declared a saint,
holed up in paradise
among the flesh-averse ascetes,
the ophanim and malachim
and the gender-neutral paraclete.

Will they have told him
the truth about love?
and has he moved on,
subsumed quite enough?

The One from Tikrit

17th December 2003

If he had tortured my father,
raped my mother,
sent my brothers to be killed in war
and cut out my tongue,
would I still pity him?
this bewildered old man,
caught in a rat-hole,
surrounded, it seems,
by American soldiers
and his own dung.

For it is surely not the same thing at all
to impose on another
what you have had to endure yourself,
an un-anaesthetised, laboratory primate
in a stall.

Plaza Mayor, Madrid

18th December 2003

Last time I was here,
it was much colder
this late in the millennial year
and the buses wore black
for those felled
in an old-style ETA attack.

The twin towers were inviolate,
apart from the truck bomb of ninety-three,
and those oil-funded faucets of gold
still belonged to that warlord,
provenance, Tikrit.

Since, we've had Ground Zero,
the Loya Jirga, Guantanamo Bay,
Weapons of Mass Destruction,
the same Saddam cooped up in gaol,
and the third partner
in this global enterprise,
no less than astonished,
democracy-era Spain,
doubled back upon itself
towards the imperial grain.
Though many things remain the same
— the autonomous nations
campaign for more independence,
corruption scandals abound —
like a fakir's pliable snake,
undreamt of economic boom
mesmerises the crowd.

It was just three months further on
that we knew:
they had their backs turned,
all of them were looking in
and nobody was watching out.

Attack

14th March 2004

All those little cafés
across from Atocha,
snug, smoky,
brown tables and chairs,
a brown counter,
the same faces every day,
for years.

Always the same order,
coffee with milk
and a pastry,
come all weathers,
all working days.

All those people
from the East and the South
taking the train
on an ordinary day.

All those staring dead,
severed heads on sleepers,
on this ordinary day.

All those winking candles,
now forever a part
of the ordinary day.

Paddy's Day

17th March 2004

Not much more than a decade ago,
we were a nation
which mainly went to Mass,
exported our youth
and remained proud
of our per capita contribution
to Live Aid.
We thought ourselves poor
but progressive,
in spite of the Church,
despite the ineptitude
of the State.

Then we had
the Brendan Smyth Affair
and the Celtic Tiger.
So ten years down the line
we've become apostate,
a nation of tribunals,
racists in Fortress Ireland,
unable to concentrate on anything
that isn't a celebrity magazine;
a Taoiseach's daughter
is now more famous
than her wheeler-dealer Dad,
and we've any amount
of teen-flesh bands
to keep our young folk blond,
buffed-up and quick-fix ambitious,
while peace abides,

in its begrudging fashion,
over the Border,
in that other part
of our hallowed land.

Dóchas linn Naomh Pádraig
Easpal Mór na h-Eireann,
hope indeed,
from the great national Apostle.
What would De Valera's Welshman
make of us now
when most of this has come and gone?

Their Day

23rd May 2015

Now over a decade further on,
two men or two women
can take each other by the hand
to be bound before this State
in matrimony,
by popular vote,
by heartfelt referendum.

As one man, not young in years,
was widely reported to have said:
'Sure, why should they be unhappy?
Let them have same chance as all of us,
for better or for worse'.

Lest We Forget...

                                                                            4th March 2017
            St Mary's, Bon Secours Mother and Baby Home, Tuam

Why would you put the body of an infant,
any mother's tender, amiable child
to rot by the side of a cesspit,
a little one who had just died?

Is it because you couldn't see
the chubby knees and ankles,
the propensity to tears and laughter,
the plasticity of that rounded head?

Is it because the only sight you beheld
was the thrusting on that night
that brought the act of lust to life
— and thought it foul as sewage?

As if Virgin was the only word you registered,
forgetting that crucial other — birth?

Children's Homes

25th May 2009

Though I was born too soon
and saved, then exiled
to an incubator,
I was cherished in rota
by each nurse whose turn
it was to be my carer,
until I became anchored, in time,
to my parents.

This gave me rights, an education,
stability and sanctuary
and that saviour cell, my hermitage,
which made an infant anchorite of me,
renouncing a world I had not seen,
receiving weekend visits through my grille
but otherwise confined to the common regime,
would in the end
permit me to prosper and roam free.

Yet still I know in my recluse soul
that one roll of the dice, that time and place
that sucks a babe from the conveyor belt,
might have sent me to the temporary hell
we now know of
as some institutional children's homes.

The Gables

14th May 2004
for Isabel Torres

My first cappuccino was in Belfast
in nineteen eighty-five.
The place, I think, was called The Gables
— favoured by the cognoscenti.

There were armoured cars on the streets
and I was fresh from the innocent West,
in the ways of this politics, dripping wet.

I was there again the other day
and the city seemed
— though made of the same red brick
and chalky grey cement —
weightless, an altogether different
kettle of fish.

D-Day, 60 Years On

31st May 2004

Young men who have never known all-out war
— though we live now in a climate of some fear —
and who have been taught to take credit
for their feeblest achievement,
to feel entitlement,
a sense of individual human worth,
cannot understand why these much older men,
their great-grandfathers,
have settled for second-fiddle lives,
living on in sufferance, as it were,
to commemorate
the better men they left behind.

The Gipper

5th June 2004
i.m. Patrick F. Sheerin

President Reagan is dead.
Ten years after his declaration of defeat,
the final one, adrift in marshes
beyond the reach of sentient time.

In Galway, in the eighties,
window frames once dark
were painted white
to show the barrel
of the putative assassin's gun;
the university Quadrangle was occupied
by boxy men in sallow macs
while graduates immolated doctorates,
degrees hard won in years
of excellence begrudged,
setting irate, futile bonfires
in the tribal city's streets.

At ninety-three,
he had no sense of having been
either actor or commander-in-chief.
What kept him alive all those years,
decerebrated in Bel Air,
must be the same
for any ordinary denizen:
an inability to die
when there is nothing left
for which to carry on.

Nancy

March 6th 2016
i.m. my mother

She died on the anniversary
of another match,
she too defined
by being a loving wife
sublimated in her husband's life.

If you had asked,
having no ambition
to claim as hers alone,
but like the blue-clad bride
on that other wedding day
— now more than half a century ago —
the new-spun wedding band
set her astride a willing horse,
one quite content
to let her have her head
and not admit its being so.

Innisfree

                                          4th August 2004

The Lake Isle of Innisfree
is more known to me
from John Ford and John Wayne
than its progenitor,
the Celtic Twilight *faber*
now casting a cold eye
on life and death
in a graveyard tourist destination
in the littoral North West.

In reality,
it looks like a Summer Pudding
afloat among several others,
low on the flat-lined horizon
and difficult to make out
from its lookalike brothers.

Last time I saw it,
on a sharp and showery evening,
there were Russians and Irish embarking
on a pre-prandial lakeshore jaunt;
new money and strangers to taste
clambering aboard a chilly,
slippery, closed-cabin launch.

Slav and Celt male,
each one red-faced,
bloated above the collar,
rough-hewn, middle-aged,
their home-grown,

honest-to-God matrons
chaffing and embarrassed
in boxy, over-tinted coiffures
and scratchy, colour-matched,
mother-of-the-bride coats,
buffalo to the geisha gazelle
from the Baltic East,
blonde locks, spray tans, bleached teeth,
gym-honed calves in four-inch heels;
either breed mere chattels,
bedecked in livery of gold,
to be traded in
or routinely ignored.

And amid this po-faced,
awkward,
unholy show,
the fabled islet
borne
cringing low.

St Stephen's Day Tsunami

> 26th December 2004

A sub-marine quake
— eight point nine on the Richter scale —
in the Indian Ocean,

eye-witness accounts
of those who fled the flaccid West
now fleeing the inexorable detritus
and the waves,

the television news absorbed by their plight:
seventy divers lost in the Emerald Caves,
journalists describing
their own and their children's
narrow escapes,

no word as yet for those
who were not on the trip of a lifetime
or a getaway Christmas break.

Car Nicobar

7th January 2005

The tectonic plates in the ocean
off Sumatra, Car Nicobar,
have brought the year
to a cataclysmic end.

With it, our phase of irrational dread
may now be dispelled,
bested by unanswerable nature,
and the rich can revert to fearing
only what wealthy ingenuity
cannot prevent.

Promenade des Anglais

14th July 2016

Now Nice has shown
that we must fear, at random,
some of our fellow men,
those left behind
in the marshes of chaos
and disorientation;
and while we,
in the uplands of well-being,
choose fabrics,
cocktails and cutlery,
consternation leads this tiny few,
these makeshift heroes,
to strike at anything
they think they cannot have,
even if that is the touch
of a little boy's podgy,
six-month-old hand.

Laois

11ᵗʰ January 2005

Overheard. A carnival Irishman declaiming today
in burnished, silver, luminous tones:
'Laois — a beautiful but neglected county'.
We were in Luton, in the departure zone.

Only the couple he bumped into and I, eavesdropping,
knew him to be, even now, the senior academic
of a onetime clandestine, maligned community.

When I was a child,
with the nation glued to the *Late Late Show*,
when Luton Airport was an impenetrable English joke,
when the furthest anyone I knew went
was not far from their own front door,
he stood up and, in that argentine voice,
he spoke.

Auschwitz Anniversary

27th January 2005

Two thirds of under thirty-fives
have never heard of it.

There have been photographs of abuse
by British soldiers in Iraq.

Under thirty-fives, perhaps.

Tracheotomy

28th February 2005

There's an old man dying in the Vatican.
He has now been deprived of his physical voice,
gone the way of the strength in his legs,
his one-time adept's balance and poise.

They say he's serene and happy,
nearing the end,
embracing all and sundry,
affirming his love.
His lungs are filling with liquid,
bringing weight to the limbs,
euphoria to the mood,
— I've seen it before,
in a less self-conscious celestial body,
a woman of the seasons and fields
who would not find offence
in such cosmology.

Some of those he leaves behind
will consider they have had
a visit from an angel,
days or weeks before
his final decline
— the soul stripped
of the trappings of life,
the ambition, the calculation,
the drive to control;
all of it incomprehensible now,
from that vantage point
beyond the impenetrable door.

April Fools' Day, Valencia

1st April 2005

'The Pope will die today'
— the newsflash interrupts
Tell Me What It Was Like,
a supersoap about the Dictatorship.
We switch from Easter Week,
Madrid, in nineteen sixty-nine
to the ailing old man in the Vatican.
Later on, you can pay for tacky shorts
and look at scrawny, naked girls
lined up like jennets in stalls
absorbing disembodied cocks,
while we have the Pope's last illness
in full view of all,
the final, choreographed image,
his back to the camera,
his face not quite yet to the wall,
looking inward, towards his creator;
this last voyage to be undertaken
without his habitual brouhaha.

I despised the spectacle of his suffering,
much as I detested his garrison mentality
mining, in those less mystical than he,
the prurience of that grinding, late-night porn.

But now, at the very end,
out of habit and courtesy,
I kneel to accompany him
on his most solitary road,
one I have been partly down myself
at least a couple of times before.

Benedict XVI

19th April 2005

According to Malachy,
you're the second last
of your kind,
you have gentle eyes
but, they say, an iron fist.

You class yourself
a simple and humble labourer
in the vineyard of the Lord,
one, however, who insists
on a silver trug, finely-worked,
to hold his garden tools.

There was a touch
of Albino Luciani about you
as you accepted,
though he, of course,
never campaigned for the post
and Giuseppe, the much disappointed
Cardinal Siri, denied his legacy,
posthumously,
to the assembled media corps.

You are said to be a transition appointment.
It seems you love music and are beloved
— yes, this is telling —
of Rome's community of feral cats.

Will you, like the last, great winter pope,
then confound us with a season of delights
— or leave us stranded on the waste ground,
thirsting still for long-lost hope?

Emeritus

11th February 2013

Did you then do more
to bestow on us that longed-for hope
by your withdrawal, than all the pomp
of wine-red, handmade loafers,
and your *mozzetta* and *camauro*,
those fur-trimmed winter capes and hats?

And are you more yourself now,
playing the piano,
communing with Contessa and Zorro,
your faithful, garden-visiting cats?

Bologna

11th September 2001
for Feargal Murray

We spent the evening
between the restaurant
and the *herboristeria*;
you bought breast-firming cream
for your ex.

That night we phoned your dad
and my mam by mobile phone,
at great expense.

It was important,
being the day the twin towers
had fallen down.

Woburn Place

8th July 2005

In a place of shrapnel,
in a place of leaves,
in a boom of teenage petulance
severed limbs among the trees,
the red bus flapping its wings
and skating on a concrete lake,
bereft of all but the sudden screams
of the mutilated and the almost dead;
in a place of manuscripts,
medicine and scholarly hush,
in a place of confluence
and intellect,
in a place of sinew, spit and bone,
private people unschooled in war
met a public end
or overt lifelong scarring.

There are, perhaps, none innocent
amongst these ordinary dead,
but unwitting, unwilling,
minding their own business, yes,
and made to pay a price
for a war they did not start
and which they have, or had,
no means of bringing to an end.

7/7

21 July 2005

July is now the cruellest month,
at least in Beeston,
ours and theirs,
and most in London,
everyone's and theirs.

A child I do not know,
the friend of a little friend's best friend
lost his father at Edgware Road,
or rather it was his father
who lost the lives of everyone else.

That little boy,
a child of grace
like any other,
will now be tarnished
forever
by his father's
and those others'
subterranean fate.

The News

5th September 2005

If you recite murder and mayhem
every day off the autocue,
if you have become inured to pictures
too awful to show to the rest of us,
if your eyeliner creates more impact
than the words you are instructed to use,
then what the hell is the point
of reading the news?

Georgie

8th December 2005
i.m. George Best

In death,
he brought an eagle-countenanced patrician
close to tears,
a man so far beyond mass-market sport
he didn't recognise the name or patient,
at first.

This was his last,
perhaps his sweetest conquest,
a hospital consultant,
in his twilight years.

This Year's Tree

18th December 2005

This year's trees are covered in carmine sparkles,
last year's were lilac and frosty white.

People are also expelling their five-year old canines
to make room for new models,
for Charpois or pups from Tibet.

Last year it was the sofa's turn,
next year the kitchen or maybe the range
will need a refresh.

Now there are hundreds of adult dogs
with nowhere to go.

Oh, and it won't be turkey this time,
they're turning to beef
because of concerns over avian 'flu.

Ten years ago, that hoof was encased
in quite a different shoe.

Ceaucescu

30th April 2006

I remember Ceaucescu dead in the snow,
then somehow I forgot
through Yugoslavia, Rwanda, Sarajevo,
right up to the Kosovar war.

God knows why,
that so-called decade of the peace dividend
seemed to pass me by.

Was it too hard to understand,
too difficult to believe,
that we had come to this
all over again?

Until September the eleventh
when we all went manic for a while,
even I, who didn't even get to see it
broadcast live.

Authority

13th June 2006
i.m. Charles Mitchell

Twenty years ago,
I wondered how I would feel
when his friendly, reptilian gaze
and cocoa vowels
finally left the screen.

His was the voice
which told us the news,
the face which made it seem real.

He retired, now he is dead,
and there are so many sources now
to be consulted and read
that it is hard to see a future
for another egg-shaped, balding head.

South Beirut

9th August, 2006
pace Robert Fisk

A single youth,
alone and defiant,
fires a rifle in the air
as he rides his motorbike
down a street in Shia South Beirut.
There's an Israeli Air Force spy plane overhead.
He has no chance of hitting it.

Shortly after,
the bombers arrive.

They leave for dead
any who may have witnessed
this headless, one-man invocation
of the gods of cyber immolation
— those aviators without eyes
zapping targets on computer screens,
a crucial fraction of a mile high
in the blue Mediterranean sky.

Mao's Long March

17th May 2007

Lost in the grasslands of the Long March,
chewing belts for sustenance,
sinking into the quagmire,
dying where they fell.

An heroic achievement
or deliberate waste
of human life?

Of ninety-seven thousand,
only six now survive.

Imagine

8th December 2007

I remember where I was
when I heard John Lennon died,
not yet twenty, way too young
to remember the Beatles
or understand why so many had to cry.

It seemed to me that he was old enough
to have lived a full and satisfying life;
but oh, a generation further on,
and it feels as if I've hardly started mine.

The Fall

6th November 2006

In a city of towers,
I overheard that twenty thousand
or more had died.
In a special edition
which might have been printed for me,
with no access at that time
to the planned-for live broadcast on TV,
a newspaper described the fall of one,
then the other vertiginous structure.

I had a plane to catch in a day or two
when the skies might be peppered
with equally noxious crew,
darting out from who knew where,
with their box-cutters
and their literal version
of truth or dare.

Little did we know
that the next crowd along
would stash bombs
beneath the soles of their feet
and deep in their groins,
sewers and sweatboxes transformed
in pursuit of an abominable desire.

Assassination

29th December 2007
i.m. Benazir Bhutto

Benazir, Benazir,
grandest of grand viziers.

The paupers of Sindh
come in their thousands
to slap their foreheads
with the heels of their hands
and tear at their flimsy clothing
as the soil arches over you
and its nakedness is clad
in the petals of a thousand roses
surprised this morning by your death,
compressed, like you,
in a sudden martyrdom,
sharing the catafalque
of upturned earth.

Benazir, Benazir,
haughtiest of haute viziers.

Hafner's Paradise

> 15th January 2008
> after Günter Schwaiger, *Hafners Paradies*, 2007.
> for Alex Coroleu

At the point of maximum stress
he removed his upper denture
wiped it with a clean handkerchief
and clicked it in again.

He repeated to the camera,
'all was propaganda':
the pyramids of bodies,
the transformation,
after two months,
of the lean to the skeletal,
the many nationalities,
the death toll in all the wars,
it all was propaganda.

He lived in a paradise
of studied compliments
paid on buses in Madrid
to unresponsive, stolid women
less than half his age.

His wrinkled, raddled face
with its porcelain white teeth
offering two for the price of one
— his carcass and that myth.

A Guest of the Bishops

Maynooth, 27th April, 2008

Like the bishops,
I haven't produced
any offspring, young tendrils
twining into the future,
at least, one supposes...

with their grave and arid mien,
these men
— were they then
the best that we could do? —
in princely silk and gold,
everyone kissing their rings,
in an age of sobriety,
a holy show,
their purpose to be bold
in the service of their king...

now interred
in a forest of tall Celtic crosses,
too close together,
forbidding and stone-cold,
while in the empty corridors
of the Victorian seminary,
their episcopal portraits
hang in testy repose;
no mothers' sons anymore
to slip on their shoes,
fill out their symbolic clothes
— the face of a scholar,
the gown of a queen...

all this long gone now
— or was it only a dream?

Intervention

30th March 2008

Five years on from the invasion of Iraq.
Back then I sat partly on the fence
— Saddam was such a monster —
and it might have worked,
along the lines of Kosova
and Sierra Leone.

But leaving the rest aside
— the lies and the paranoia,
small footprint, big boots
and a people restored to themselves
in the Garden of Eden —
the fact is
the site of the Great Flood,
the lozenge of the Tigris
and the Euphrates,
is all spattered now,
drenched in arterial blood.
The creatures of Noah,
the children of the Ark,
blown to smithereens
around a military game park.

Harry Patch

26th July 2009

He died yesterday
at the age of one hundred and eleven.
At twenty-one a German shell at Passchendaele
ripped his stomach apart
and he lay for thirty-six hours
in un-anaesthetised pain
until a doctor cut the shrapnel out
and sutured him with four men holding him down.

That gave him ninety further years,
for seventy-nine of which,
like all his generation, he thought he had no choice
but to keep his mouth shut and carry on.
A long, an uneventful life, it was,
until he became the last man alive
to survive the Somme.

He said then
that war was no more than 'organised slaughter',
murder by government-purchased bullet and gun.
Uniqueness, longevity, isolation
brought authority to this simple statement,
Passchendaele, in its time,
not seeming statement enough.

Stevo

10th October 2009
i.m. Stephen Gately

Is it easy to mourn a man of thirty three?
— we have wept for one for twenty centuries.
Did he die too on the hurdle of fame,
turned sour by notoriety and shame?

There was, indeed, for each,
an interlude of wilderness,
Gethsemane, despair,
but attributed miracles, contrived or not,
maybe left them both surprised,
if they were inward, unassuming,
though all the while
enslaved by the instinct to display.

His was the modern testament of words and music
construed, by those with more at stake,
as longed-for prophecy, the ending of the wait,
projected from afar on the soccer stadium stage.

Another Thirty-Three

13th October 2010

Up from the bowels of the earth,
half a mile through gold-flecked stone
beneath the Atacama desert
and before the cameras of the world,
in parchment:
'We are well in the refuge,
the thirty-three'.

After seventeen days of facing death,
and forty-two of nursing hope
and caring for each other,
each one arrives like an astronaut
freed from the nether regions of despair.
And while the day produces startling glare,
with thousands more to follow it,
benevolent and some inevitably sad,
they are safe, just that,
because once in the rising capsule
they could not bend again to look back.

And there was no bargain,
only good luck after bad.

Traitor in Gaza

24th November 2012

Christ has not been crucified
and died to save us all
if a man with his face, his skin,
his beard, his genes,
perhaps — although we'll never know —
his innocence,
can be dragged through the streets,
in nothing but a makeshift loincloth,
chased in blood and marked
by the signs of torture,
his corpse yoked to the wheels
of two throbbing motorbikes,
where once, we are told,
a woman wiped Christ's face
so he could see
and a man shouldered his cross
to ease the crushing burden
of that tree and his sacrifice.

Nothing has been gained
— such a hopeless thing, I know, to say
and likely not my place.

The Children of Gaza

27th January 2009
for Penny Aldred

I
One was struck by lightning on a golf course
and survived.
She saw King George V's crown tumble from his coffin
and told the tale.
She kept a diary all the years her husband was away
in the Second Great War.
She endured long enough to become bereft of wind and
                                                                           limb,
recollection or present mind,
enough to become a toddler to her own child,
herself a long while retired.

II
At ninety-five, another was still driving, baking, opining,
still in a vintage cottage with a blooming garden,
still climbing stairs and keeping windows ajar,
eschewing radiators, sitting on hard chairs.
When her time came — and she chose it —
she went from ambulance to death
in a matter of forty-eight hours.
So neat and tidy was her passing,
as if accelerating down the hill
in the Micra she drove to her dying day,
that no-one noticed it
between Christmas lunch and afternoon tea.

III
As these doughty women take their leave
there are all those children pulverized

in the ruins of Gaza...
those ninety years they witnessed and survived
have left no trace, it seems,
at least, not to any observer's naked eye.

Plenipotentiary

I often tell the cat that we are lucky:
plenty to eat, good flavours,
soft places to sleep.

We treat each other lovingly,
at least most of the time,
speak in soft tones
— we even have check-ups for our teeth.

But every night we witness
such atrocities
— that is, I do, she pretends to sleep —
rape, torture, wilful starvation.

There is always a manicured,
shifty-eyed ambassador
primed to deny it,
addressing the demagogues
of his own nation
via our mainstream, terrestrial TV.

Desperate
— like all common rodents,
she later tells me —
to avoid his own,
or his family's,
impending immolation.

II

'While the earth remaineth, seed-time and harvest
shall not fail.'

Thanksgiving for the Blessings of Harvest,
Common Prayer.

Words and Music

> Murroogh Mountain, Co. Clare,
> Church of St Ilan, Mynydd Eglwysilan, Aber Valley, Wales.
> i.m. Tom Breathnach

Murroogh Mountain,
with nestled houses, glistening slates,
chimney smoke on its slabbed face,
an M visible, in most lights,
from across the bay;
my province of Munster conspiring
with the forsaken one above,
a line of faith astride
bridging all the tides
and urging me:
it would not be
overweening to write.

Though then it took
an unconscionable time
for me to realise
that the artisan's tools
were mine by right.

Eglwysilan Mountain,
the church on an early pilgrim route
and the opposite lip of its farming valley
dotted with snow-white chalets,
redress for the slag heap
when mining ceased — and left
the stone-clad village below it bereft,
suspicious of strangers,
turned in on itself.
I'd come to my quartile of maisonette
in hope, yet welcome

from those Cambrian shores
was tardy, too late to block the impetus
of the border-bound removals men.

I still regret the long and sloping garden,
tuned in, had I only known it,
to the mists, the stones
and the resonant air.

Newstead Abbey

> Augustinian Canons' Priory of St Mary, 1170,
> Newstead, Nottinghamshire,
> re-modelling post-1818, John Shaw Sr.

That façade, Gothic tracery
buttressed against thin air,
against a backdrop
of peacock-blue sky
and luxuriant, bell-shaped
demesne trees,
with the mewling cries of April livestock
placid in a fragrant breeze,
the people in their cotton prints
taking cream teas,
displaying a matter-of-fact grasp
of local history.

Here were gentry families
succeeding each on each,
none lasting long enough
to fill the breach forged
when the canons were dethroned,
and thus when Byron played
and loved and wrote,
and other mundane things besides,
the abbey had no refuge for his pilgrim soul;
no dog, no man, no flesh, no fowl,
no creed of reason
nor lightening flash of his intensity
could restore the symmetry that was made
when they first erected
that façade.

But in the gardens, the apothecary

— away from that austerity,
and the later pseudo-Gothic,
quasi-Pugin, hyper-crenellated rooms —
with bloom of shrub and flower,
with stench of stagnant water, pungent herb
and horse-dung on the earth
here were signs,
an extant line
of lore and ancestry.

Acre

> Cluniac Priory of St Mary, 1100-1150,
> Castle Acre, Norfolk.

Softer than you'd expect,
the patterns on the original walls,
flint in the beehive mounds
the texture and colour of tweed,
buttressed with affable gargoyles.

Land that was worked by monks
long left to grass and hedgerow,
a chorus of self-contained, elderly trees
all that remains of the daughter
of the first Cluniac settlement in England.

The Prior's Lodging
became a farmer's house
when surrendered
to the bigamous king.
The abbey, first looted,
was left to rot by its side,
its roof and cloisters
by dint of royal ordnance
symbolically destroyed.

It was, indeed,
not always a pious place,
before or after Cistercian reform,
but once there was awareness of beauty
and striving in a spiritual mode.

Clonmacnoise

> Monastery of Clonmacnoise, founded by St Ciaran, 545,
> Clonmacnoise, Co. Offaly.

Three wise men on the base
of the east face
of the Cross of the Scriptures,
part of what remains of Celtic Christianity
in the parish of Clonfert.

Vikings, Normans
and miscreant Irish
used to sail up the Shannon
with regularity, to sack the monastery
and its church.

Every time, the brothers rebuilt,
until fifteen fifty-two,
when roofless ruins were all
the boy king Edward's Athlone garrison
left.

Seán Buí

Dromoland Castle, Co. Clare,
original late fifteenth-century tower house erected
by Thomas MacAnerheny,
re-built in the present baronial style
by James and George Richard Pain, 1835.

It was supposed to be a hermit's cell
placed on the edge of a marshy pool,
though it was difficult to picture,
even then when we took such things
literally for granted,
how a human could withstand
the dankness, the sharpness,
the stagnant, putrid smell.

The little temple, on the other hand,
was set upon a neatly-landscaped mound
with winding avenues from the castle
down to the tonsured, artificial pond.
A tiny Eros on a Grecian dome,
beneath it lay Seán Buí
who won an all-or-nothing bet
to save both villagers and tenants
from his raucous lordship's
overweening gambling debt.

In the same bounds,
by the paving-slab promontory
and the sun-dial in the lily fronds:
the dissolution of a rackrent aristocracy
and the apotheosis of the early Faith
— or how a racehorse saved
these hotel grounds,
this one-time Henrician
Surrender-and-Regrant estate.

Little Things

> Jean-Baptiste-Camille Corot, *Marsh at Arleux*, 1871,
> National Gallery, London.

One of the smallest pictures
hung in a room
dominated by an Ingrès
of a florid woman
in a chintz-patterned dress
and a large-format sequence,
by Corot himself,
of morning, noon, evening and night,
describing the arc of light,
with a peasant as focal point,
a blood-red kerchief
round his labouring head:
a late work,
the *Marsh at Arleux*, northern France.

Anon the curators,
middle-aged men in their navy blazers,
idly discussing Shakespeare,
while the vaguely bohemian young
slowly throng around the Millets
and a Rosa Bonheur
of masterful steeds at market
she had to research
by dressing as a man.
Not a patch on it,
a ponderous narrative of death at sea
by a painter who spent
many days making studies
in the Dutch village of Zandvoort.

Beside them, this little Corot
of the marsh at Arleux
in which there is no human figure
to draw in the eye,
in which he scratched out the reeds
with the wooden point
at the end of the handle
of his artist's brush.

We might think it had been vandalised
if history and provenance
had not vouchsafed us that much.

A Beach in Fife

                      Jack Vettriano, *The Singing Butler*, 1992.

A couple waltz on a flat beach
before a foaming, windblown sea.
They've brought a maid and a butler
to brace umbrellas,
useless against the breeze.

The men are stark in black,
the women in a dash of red
— the careworn, hat-clamped servants' heads,
the slender backs of the well-off necks,
their ballroom-stiff, averted glances,
tuxedoed beau and bias-cut lady
play-acting romance on a water-logged strand
yet thoroughgoing strangers
to make-believe, Tinseltown dance.

Bonnington

> Richard Parkes Bonnington, *Fishmarket*, 1824,
> Yale Center for British Art, New Haven, CT;
> Joaquín Sorolla y Bastida, *Boys on the Beach*, 1910,
> Prado Museum, Madrid.

Bonnington, like Sorolla,
is to do with light.
But not a mottled, dazzling,
sand-papered kind
with boys like seals on beaches,
all roughened skin
and bulging eyes, teeth and smiles;
rather the quiet luminescence
of workaday seashore life:
an amber-coloured sail on a barge,
a creel of fish, a mended net,
and always an expanse of brightness,
like a translucent veil
cast over fisherfolk, sea and sky.

The Venice of Savoy

Alfred-Henri Recoura,
The Basilica of the Visitation, 1909-1930, Annecy.
i.m. Lucie Couprie

Saint François de Sales and Sainte Jeanne de Chantal,
founders together of the Order of the Visitation,
celebrated in a basilica on the side of a hill
in Annecy, the Venice of Savoy,
surrounded by Alps, skiing, chamoix,
marmottes, puck goats, St Bernards and,
at land level, cafés, canals, expensive shops,
knick-knacks, holidaymakers in shorts,
eating ice-creams, drinking wine and beer on terraces,
against the backdrop of the former prison
on an island in the middle of one of the waterways
garrisoned with trompe l'oeil children's attractions.

All well and good.
We are so lucky
to live as we do,
and yet...
people are so very busy now
with accountability.
The labour-saving devices
thrown up by the last century
have left time which is being used
to itemise dishonesty,
to clamour for the meanest
of undelivered consumer rights.
Take the basilica.

It was closed when I went up the hill today,
though it is a site of pilgrimage
and it was not an easy climb.

I assume the religious were
enveloped in prayer
and did not wish to be distracted
so turned unlooked-for custom,
absent-mindedly, away.
I could have demanded
an apology, a making of amends,
but would that not have been
an insult to their truth?

Despite my disappointment then
and the fact that it is unlikely
I will ever come this way again,
I went back down that steep path
to the heat of the canals,
the backdrop of the blue Alps,
and the hum of secular quietude.

Spire

> Ian Ritchie Assoc./Arup, *The Spire of Dublin*, 2003.

The steel spire in O'Connell Street
catches all the tones of light,
like an East Window.

A cathedral which takes up
almost no space
and has no orthodoxy.

Pilgrimage

> Church of St Columba,
> Drumcliffe, Co. Sligo.

Seven years ago,
before the renovation,
I recognised the church, the pennants, the place,
the names of families and gentility long gone,
the seed which sprang those Butler Yeats
— much venerated, mystical race —
athwart the sphinx of Ben Bulben.

Now, in the new timber of restoration,
all seems, freshly, undone.

Portico

> Marià Fortuny i Marsal, *Nude on the Beach at Portici*, 1874,
> Prado Museum, Madrid.

This painter died
at thirty-six,
thirteen days
after he finished a work
which might have been
a new beginning.
Nobody knows quite why
he had to meet his end,
only he recognised, it seems,
the time had come
though he then had
two young children
and, it appears,
a beautiful wife,
rather *spirituelle*.

To leave
so very, very soon,
and less in thrall to masters
and the market
than heretofore;
looking to a future,
with that naked, austere bather
on a shore
in Portici,
vouchsafing us a portal
we would never,
at least by his hand,
come to know
or even begin to comprehend.

Veneziana

Right beside you,
their clumsy, chomping kisses
smacking in your ear,
juvenile tourists
with their many-tongued
endearments elbow in
and lean, their backs
against the parapet
and the Rialto sky,
to be photographed
for posterity.

Then they move on,
that job done,
to the next
anthologised site,
a shot of their torsos entwined
as they pass beneath
the long-suffering Bridge of Sighs.

All these infant souls
blinded, maybe lamed,
by the requirement
— a constant —
to project,
befuddled by a world
that gives no licence to explore
those things that cannot be uploaded
to an insubstantial, odourless core.

Turner in Venice

> J.M.W. Turner,
> *The Interior of San Marco, Looking into the North Transept,*
> 1840, Tate Gallery, London.

Many churches in the Eastern Rite
have mosaics and dark-hued,
saucer-eyed madonnas.
St Mark's has these
and nonchalant, chatting workmen
up on platforms preparing for Christmas
and Western Celebration,
when the Patriarch will stand,
his feet on the three-tiered ambo,
his head under its golden, miniature dome
and preach, as all have done before him,
not least, the twinkling Pope
of those thirty-three spellbound days
in August and September, nineteen seventy-eight.

Tourists will continue to queue
and enter this most talked-about of shrines
only to emerge disappointed,
not having expected it to be
so dark inside, so hazy on the eye.

Yet, only one hundred and fifty years before,
Turner, to whom the sun's great light was all,
fathomed, by its seeming absence
in that redolent, bejewelled vault,
so much of succour to the human soul.

Stratford

A man who wrote for a living,
did some acting too,
maybe a bit of entrepreneurship.

His bones lie in the parish church,
rather high, of course, lit at night,
and the graveyard's well-manicured,
as are the houses down the road,
some of them electric-gated even.

Of the crowds of tourist pilgrims,
like well-laundered sheep,
who start with the birthplace
and finish with the resting-place,
very many would barely recognise
a word of what he generated,
being merely the cash crop
in the moneytrap in-between.

A Room in the Prado, Now Dispersed

> Tiziano Vecellio, *Charles V at Mühlberg*, 1548;
> Pieter Pawel Rubens, *The Duke of Lerma on horseback*, 1603;
> Pieter Pawel Rubens,
> *The Cardinal-Infante Don Fernando at Nördlingen*, 1634;
> Diego de Silva y Velázquez,
> *The Count-Duke of Olivares on horseback*, 1636.

A warrior emperor, plumed in dusky pink,
with jutting chin and finely armoured bone,
his stallion compact and collaborative,
the lance in his right hand, sceptre and throne.

A soft-eyed duke on a Venusian unicorn,
all flowing mane and silken tail,
the melting eyes of man and beast
no harbinger of his final, judicial betrayal.

A cardinal, but not a priest, with the face
and milky sweetness of a child,
confident astride a nervy, anxious steed,
then undermined and driven to an early grave.

A swarthy plenipotentiary,
his shining chestnut high in muscular levade,
a count-cum-duke disgraced just two years on
and banished to his out-of-town estate.

Is there a lesson to be learned
from these four riders so seigniorially arrayed?
Or is it the horses, one angelic,
who tell us what these painters actually displayed?

Dublin Grey

> After Géricault, *A Horse*,
> National Gallery of Ireland, Dublin.

A pale horse
on a dark ground
sent by post
to a recipient
who may not have understood
that, giddy and dishevelled,
she might have been ridden by Oisín
across all the waves
from here to Tír na n-Óg,
then been astounded
by the hard road
so blithely undertaken;

horrified because she knew
there would be no way home
for the horseman so mundanely fallen
while picking up a stone
amounting to a boulder
to the midgets he encountered
as his grey first glided ashore
after what he — but not she —
had understood to be
a furlough spent abroad.

No, the recipient will not need to be told
anything more
than its being a painting
after the style
of Théodore Géricault.

Rupprecht and Fergal

> SS. Rupprecht and Vergilius,
> St Andrew's Church, Salzburg.
> with thanks to Veronika Oberparleiter Coroleu

Rupprecht, of Frankish royal blood,
a tiny, dusky madonna and child
in the palm of his left hand
— the lady of Altötting —
and a barrel by his feet,
for he was a miner of salt
as well as heathen souls.

Fergal, his successor, of the line
of Niall of the Nine Hostages born,
a maquette of the cathedral
sitting on his right,
his crozier tilting towards the sky
— for he was an astronomer —
on the other side.

Both prelates almost taking off,
airborne missionaries from another time,
their backs to the present post-war altar,
the church they had been sculpted for
torn down over a century ago
to make way for a new road.

When the neo-Gothic alternative
in a new location
was only half that century old
anschluss, blitzkrieg,
Armageddon,
Coventry and Dresden
fell out of the heavens

and that church was, in its turn,
collaterally destroyed,
though then amended, not re-constructed,
and the Gothic Revival altarpiece
replaced — going further back —
by a neo-Byzantine cross
set against smudgy East Window stained glass.

There are two black and white photos at the side
showing the *Andräkirche* as it once was,
with those windblown baroque bishops on pilasters,
clad in mitres and copes of molten gold.

Rock of Ages

Notre Dame de Bon-Espoir,
Church of Notre Dame, c. 1220, Dijon.

Three Wise Men,
or maybe a Trinity,
as if wind had carved them
on a golden rock
then blown it, an erratic,
to the edge of the choir,
above the crossing of this nave,
to catch the rose light of the transept
from the waxing and the waning day;
a sixties Gaulish altar block
in the shrine of an apocryphal madonna
restored to show a Roman polychrome face.

She saw off pestilence and military plague
as recently as nineteen forty-four
and now bedecked for Easter
in starched, embroidered linen,
this Lady of Good Hope,
older and wiser than her advocation,
listens as the elderly devout of Dijon
come up and bless themselves,
then kneel and pray.

Gabriel

> Cathedral of the Peak,
> Church of St John the Baptist, Tideswell, Derbyshire.
> i.m. Joanna Turner

The angel Gabriel of the Peak
is cool of mien
and sallow of face,
aloof in Victorian chastity,
androgynous in grace.

His hair is blond
and bound by a diadem,
his robe is turquoise blue
with golden trim,
and his wings, though folded,
are fair and intact,
tethered behind him
to his perch
on the re-plastered apse.

The attitude is one of forbearance
and prayer,
as though there were
suppressed pain,
something chaffing him
in that posture,
while seeming to hang
blithe and content
from a spancel in the air.

Church Militant

> Standing Buddhas, c. 4th Century, Bamiyan, Afghanistan;
> Cluniac Priory of St Mary, 1100-1150, Castle Acre, Norfolk.
>
> for Elizabeth Taylor

We rail against the Taliban
for blowing up the Buddhas of Bamiyan,
but what the Anglicans did here
in their tertiary year
left only the west façade
and a rockery of flints
occasionally glowing
with warm-toned marble hints,
as the window glass
was once emblazoned by the setting sun.

The monks thrown out on the roads
to beg for crumbs
in a world they had long ago abjured,
promised pensions callously unpaid,
and some, innocents unwilling to resort to less
than oration and penitence,
hearts still trained on the world as yet to come,
fated to deposit their miserable ossuaries
on the banks of those self-same thoroughfares
where once they had offered well-intentioned,
communal prayers.

Eyeless and unglazed,
that west façade,
beloved of Romantic artists,
then cleaned and blanketed
in lush green sward,
— downier than anything
those monks had known

in their roughspun habits
and unforgiving dormitory boards,
lovelier perhaps than the heaven
they had imagined —
that remnant left deliberately to show
the might of the recusant monasteries
broken on the wheel
and marketed now,
like the strawberry jam
sold in miniature pots,
in a children's adventure day spiel.

Destiny

> Velázquez and workshop,
> *The Archduchess Maria Anna, Queen of Spain*, 1653,
> Kunsthistorischesmuseum, Vienna.

Poor, pudding-faced dumpling,
wedded to her pasty-hued uncle,
his second bride,
downturned lips,
vacant, worried eyes
beneath a dense, be-ribboned wig,
her face the cavemouth
in a muddy, low-slung hill,
as broad across her narrow head
as the cartwheel farthingale,
flat and wide,
that *guardainfante* skirt,
for a time
associated with offspring
from the sinister side,
set here astride those milch-cow hips,
apparatus to provide
the moribund family
with a prince.

Summoned to foal a colt
to fill the Madrid throne
she duly brought forth a pair,
her firstborn with the sacred disease
who would not live
to be the failing Empire's
new-found Hercules,
the second inheriting child,
another Charles, as much desired,
with turquoise eyes and long, fair hair,

a willing heart
yet instability of mind
and no capacity to walk
without leaning on a man or wall,
a king, in sum, who might not rule.

No wonder Velázquez saw
in their mother's gaze
so much bewilderment of pain,
eight years before this final birth.
A widow, she went on,
as regent to her ailing scion,
to don a monochrome nun's robe,
appropriate the throne, endure...
this sad-eyed Madonna
at the end of the Madrid branch
of the Habsburg line.

Discovery

> Discalced Carmelite Monastery of Our Lady of Pity,
> 1594, Cascais, Portugal.

On the edge of the known world,
though all were aware of the voyages,
the requirement to accept
and, if necessary, re-think
what had always been
incontrovertible truth;

in a new house, prepared for austerity,
lives of candid prayer,
that bet taken on the soul's survival,
an eternity in comfort, ecstasy even,
at the cost of unremitting carnal ache;

these monks gathered in the carcass
of what would be their everyday church,
sang the Eucharist into its skeleton joists,
and opened a school to mould novices
into men of contemplation like themselves.

The foundation offset the squat,
strategic fortress across the square
— the law of Mars much longer entrenched
than that of the Discalced Carmel.
In silent Christian colloquy,
there was to be a female establishment,
never built, somewhere above
that stretch of lustrous beach,
at best a mere resource
to all those kneeling men
absorbed, with *cilis* or *flagellum*,

in the discipline
of their own indentured flesh.

Yet aboriginal nakedness,
in Summer thrall
to Dionysius and Apollo,
in time, would utterly forestall
that headway so exquisitely acquired
through flick of whip
and stroke of credent pen.

The Stars Look Down

                        King St Stephen (Istvan Kiraly), 1906;
    Frigyes Schulek, Fishermen's Bastion (Halaszbastya), 1895-1902;
      Imre Steindl, Hungarian Parliament (Országház), 1885-1902.

On the Pest side
— an overcast sky and rain —
bulletholes in the cornerstones
which have withstood
over seventy years,
first Goulash Communism,
then Velvet Revolution
followed by the tourist boom.
Stag and hen parties
— invasions of the barely-clothed
from the thriving west and north —
staggering round the level streets
as if they were merely revelling
on cheaper shots and beer
than they could purchase at home.

With the moon on his shoulder
— purplish clouds on a blue ground —
his back to the Enlightenment he did not know
and the subsequent parliament
for all those tongues and would-be nations
then amputated in nineteen eighteen,
King Szent István up in Buda
watches the wheel
as it turns yet another degree,
recalling the Pagan lord, Vata
who shaved his head but for three long tresses
so he could be the torment
of Stephen's newborn Christianity.
Now, the half-clad hordes

from the west and north
have little or none
of the same sense of certainty.

The Gellért

>   Ármin Hegedüs, Artúr Sebestyén and Izidor Sterk,
>   Hotel Gellért, 1912-1918;
>   Freedom Bridge (Franz Josef Bridge), János Feketeházy,1894-96;
>   Liberty Statue, Zsigmond Kisfaludi Strobl, 1947.

It was finished the year my father was born,
the year of the Armistice,
the year the Empire was torn asunder
and the lower lands fell away
into the post-Ottoman Balkans.

In the western part, Spanish 'flu
laid waste to the Habsburg seat,
cut off Schiele in his
bony, introverted prime
and before him, smock-clad,
Byzantine Gustav Klimt,
maker of liquid, erotic mosaics;
the same venomous decline
made off with an infant uncle of mine,
one my gestating father
would only be able to view
in a formal portrait
taken in a run-of-the-mill
photographer's studio.

This palace emerged,
in style late Secessionist, Art Nouveau,
perched on the nap of the slope
from which the Venetian Gerardo,
Benedictine and bishop,
Szent Gellért to be in his adopted abode,
was tied to a chariot and cast
down towards the Danube a millennium before;
his grave much later spanned

by the Belle Époque Franz Josef bridge
and his martyrdom tagged
— inadvertently? —
by the Iron Curtain Liberty Monument
resurgent on the brow of the hill.

Acts of faith in better times ahead:
the bridge after Austro-Hungary
had dissolved
to release the Magyar throne;
the hotel, before and after that terrible war
which left no wrong undone
and sowed the seeds
of far worse yet to come;
the Soviet victor's palm leaf held aloft,
like a cross on Gellért Hill,
a prelude to Gethsemane
and four decades of internment,
now long gone.

Those hoped-for better times?
My father, if alive,
would nearly be a centenarian,
but with razor-wire fences
girding the border to repel not contain,
that near namesake Gerardo
might never have relinquished
— learned, hospitable island —
his monastery of San Giorgio
all those long centuries ago.

Sentries

> Saddell Abbey, founded by Somerled, 1160
> (Clan MacDonald, Lords of the Isles),
> Kintyre Peninsula, Argyll and Bute.

Sitting out the word of God,
these sons of Malachy,
the saint of Mellifont
who crossed the sea
and discovered the green lake;
his last foundation
beside a coursing stream,
a glen, a wood
— the cold on their unshod feet,
disease-ridden livestock in the fields...

later, knights in stone
carved in the Kintyre style,
effigies of faceless Scots,
more Norman
than the Normans themselves,
strewn up and down
the Western Isles,
perennially damp,
in post for centuries
along the Atlantic coast
— warriors wind-surfing
on the breath of the Lord.

III

'as thy holy Angels always do thee service in heaven,
so by thy appointment they may succour and defend
us on earth;'

Collect for the Feast of St Michael and All Angels,
Common Prayer.

Sunflowers

A man in a butcher's striped apron,
close-cropped hair,
sunburnt neck,
love-handles swelling above the belt,
the look of someone intent...

on piling sunflowers, carnations,
pert-eyed, innocent, erect,
chrysanthemum bouquets
in polythene wrap,
on a pyre...

he thinks he's burning rubbish
in a rusty barrel, fire
in the rag-tag hole...

but on a pristine sky-blue morn
I see consternation
in a builder's yard in Kent.

Actor

A dangling penis
glimpsed between the two skulls
in the seats in front,
sheltered by a clutched sheet
from the public in the stalls
— we caught it in silhouette,
from our seats down the side,
a bit-part player, a non-speaking role,
eyeing us with a timid glance,
afraid to raise its cautious,
snake-like head too high
before that sea of would-be
avid, unforgiving eyes.

The Higher Forms

An elfin soprano
raised off the rake to the lid
of an upright piano,
as if she weighed
no more than a melting flake
of diaphanous snow.

A dancer, silent in basque,
suspenders and brassière,
looking as if all he did was wave
to get her there.

These are bargains made
with the lives we lead
behind the pupils of our eyes
and in the antechambers
on the other side of sleep.

Waltz

His hand on my spine
wrapped like fog around a lamp-post,
the colour and intoxication of wine.

A portal revealing itself from behind,
the trap-door to a spiral stairway,
the clang of foot on metal,
silken infiltration of the mind.

In the light of day
the golden shadows still persist,
billow and snap like sheets in the wind,
a falling motion, like a swoon.

Let me now unfasten
the front door in the ordinary way
and let him in.

Releasing

Out of the white box
comes a single flower
in monochrome,
green the first time,
blue the second.
No more than a simple line,
a series of buttons
on a ladies' lace-up shoe,
pencilled eyebrows,
drooping-tassel moustaches,
insect-wings in flight,
a maze of starbursts:
two portraits
in almost black-and-white.

Lost at Sea

If death calls you,
must you go?
drawn to the crashing waves,
oblivious of the plunging cliffs,
like a merman
summoned to the deep,
away from this ten-toed world
that would not let you breathe?

You might like to know
— and I am a stranger —
that plastic flowers
and a limestone seat
mark your passing,
put there for those who walk
on ten-toed feet.

The Bosphorus

With each breath
you surfaced again from drowning,
the Herculean effort of grasping once more
your fragile purchase on life.
This with every succeeding intake of air
over a period of several hours,
so much that the six-pack of your abdomen
might have been the pride of long months
of crunches and sit-ups,
muscle-building supplements
and water deprivation,
though yours was the fruit of a short few days
of self-resuscitation, each effort deeper
into your ribcage than your healthy body
would have dreamt it could endure,
your determination to overcome, to survive
transcending all the habitual limitations
of your being, unready to relinquish
the burden of being alive.

And yet depart you did,
like Leander on the Bosphorus
bagged at last by unanswerable fatigue,
but unlike him, shepherded to your new life
by Hero's voice and her caress,
for she understood
that you no longer had
the gift of sight
in those tawny, sea-green eyes.

Love

> i.m. Nellie Geraghty,
> d. 24th November 2011.

She was killed for her handbag,
clumsily and inadvertently,
by a man who had been addicted as long
as her husband had not been alive.

The man needed money
to pay drug debt or ease that urge.
All he saw was fair game,
easy pickings. So he made a lunge

and she hung on, fell, bumped her head.
At seventy-nine a tumble
she would not survive,
bringing an end to a dogged, bereft life,

crossed with heroism of an uncommon kind.
In the bag was a phial of his ashes.
She had not suffered him once to leave her side,
and for that honour bond, she was ready to die.

Generations

All told, it was a noble death,
that fine-boned, taciturn man
in his tenth decade,
and you nearly at the end of your fifth;

the fulcrum moving along so it sits now
between your children and you,
the balance tipped for these years to come
by your hand,

until the day
your strength no longer holds
the see-saw from its sway.

Remnants

>for Linda Hart

In the islands of the night
there are ghosts,
if truth be told.

Mostly it is not,
and they remain
unharvested, unaneeled.

Sevvy

> Severiano Ballesteros Sota,
> 9th April 1957–7th May 2011.

My father loved him.
Sevvy.
The first Spanish name
he ever pronounced
and so outlandish:
Severiano.
And the surname was just as bad:
Ballesteros.
Not exactly ready-made for fame,
like Arnold Palmer, say,
a good brandy
and mellifluous on the tongue,
or Christy O'Connor Senior,
a glass of Paddy
with a porter chaser,
but Severiano Ballesteros!
How in the name of God
could he roll his lips around that one?

And yet,
from doe-eyed, fulminant youth,
to tortured, cantankerous decline,
we loved no-one as much,
not even, these days,
that poor, bedevilled Tiger Woods.

For all I know,
my father, who predeceased him
while he was in his sporting prime,
might have glimpsed the destined truth

above the blinding, megawatt smile,
the pain that would take up residence
— eventually —
behind those haunted, chestnut eyes.

Rugby For Your Country

Those great, big, meaty men
clashing like tanks
and racing like mail-clad gazelles
with hands as delicate as new-laid eggs,
and eyes apt to prick with tears
at the beginning and end of it all,
offsetting the bulging scars,
the cauliflower ears
and the hesitant recall.

Catnap

The curve of her back
in the cove of my hip,
that rumble in her ribs
we do not understand
— conferring the essence of eternity
in a single moment...

holding its purity of line
amid the querulous calls
from what has been left unsatisfied
along the slow ellipse of time.

Monsters

The ends of the earth
are not to be feared,
they are earth only
and the doings of humanity.

The treads of eternity, however,
present a different matter.
Air and nothingness,
a parabola of finality.

16.06.2012

A sort of symmetry of sixes
makes today's date;
also Bloomsday.

Quill

Never face a blank page
until you know
that with your ink
you have plans
to desecrate
the untrodden
snow.

Advice from the children's laureate,
Michael Morpurgo.

Edna O'Brien

'I am come of fierce people',
she said,
in that carefully modulated
emigrant accent;
a snapshot taken
on the day she left
Tuamgraney, East Clare,
coated here and there
with drawling overtones,
slack-jawed vowels
and blade-sharp consonants,
making her a creature
of there and nowhere,
the hull of once monotoned,
narrow-beamed, childhood articulation
encrusted with voices
like cabauchon barnacles,
carrying her a long way
from Clare to here.

Imbolc

for Lorna Shaughnessy

Today, I'm told,
is Imbolc,
the feast of St Bridget,
the women's saint
— men have so many;
the one who understands
from her outpost
on the druidic margins,
the edge of life,
the hemline of the sea;
a state to which
we must all pay homage,
if we can,
on bended knee.

Also by Jean Andrews

Poetry
In an Oubliette
Lunatica
Sí-Orphans of the Plaintive Air
The Heron on the Lake

Translations
Nancy Morejón, Black Woman and Other Poems
Carmen Conde, While the Men Are Dying
Eibhlín Dhubh Ní Chonaill, The Lament for Arthur O'Leary (in *Sí-Orphans*)

www.ingramcontent.com/pod-product-compliance
Lightning Source LLC
Chambersburg PA
CBHW071703040426
42446CB00011B/1898